# 50 IN 50.

## BY T.J. ROHLEDER
### AKA AMERICA'S
### BLUE JEAN MILLIONAIRE

"<u>50</u> of the Greatest Things Learned in My First <u>50</u> Years of Life and How They May Be Vital to Your Success."

FIRST EDITION

ISBN-10: 1-933356-24-3
ISBN-13: 978-1-933356-24-2

Edited & Designed by Chris Bergquist

Printed in the United States of America

Dear Friend,

This small book contains 100 of the very best ideas I have ever learned about success and money. I hope you enjoy and prosper greatly from them.

To celebrate my 50th birthday, I thought it would be a fun idea to put together a list of my 50 greatest money-making secrets I have learned in my first 50 years of life! Well, I couldn't stop at 50 secrets. Besides, one of the greatest secrets I've learned is to always strive to give people more!

So, in the spirit of giving more – and to celebrate my 50th birthday by giving you more – I offer these 100 powerful ideas to you. ENJOY!

Sincerely,

T.J. Rohleder
www.RuthlessMarketing.com

# There are only 3 ways to build a business:

1. Get more customers.

2. Sell more high-ticket items – for bigger profits.

3. Sell more often to your customers!

---

**Almost all million-dollar marketing ideas are transferable from one business to another.**

---

**50 IN 50.**

Selling is the art of
proving that what
you have to offer is
worth far, far MORE
than the money they
must give up.

**50 IN 50.**

# CREATE *IRRESISTABLE* OFFERS!

**"I want to create offers that are like heads of fresh lettuce that are thrown into a pen of starving rabbits!"**

*(I wrote this in 1997.)*

# 50 IN 50.

# Think on paper!

The very act of
putting your ideas
on paper forces
you to think!

**50 IN 50.**

\* \* \* \* \*

# *Blur* the lines between your work and play.

\* \* \* \* \*

**50 IN 50.**

# The power of the 5 A.M. Club:

- Force yourself to get out of bed before you want to – and put on a big pot of strong black coffee. – Pull out some paper and pens and start writing!

- Ideas <u>will</u> come to you and through you – that you would <u>never</u> have discovered <u>if</u> you stayed in bed!

There is a magic at work here that's hard to explain!  You must experience it – <u>before</u> you can believe it!

**50 IN 50.**

# Less is more.

It's far better to be a
master at 2 or 3 things –
than to be average at doing
a whole bunch of things.

# 50 IN 50.

\* \* \*

The real business
is  between our ears
and in our hearts –
*not in the office!*

\* \* \*

**50 IN 50.**

$ $ $

A strong <u>risk-reversal</u> <u>offer</u> takes a lot of courage, but this can make you **<u>super rich</u>**!

$ $ $

# 50 IN 50.

"I have a lot of competition, but <u>ZERO</u> competitors!"

*Kerry Thomas*

**50 IN 50.**

$ $ $ $ $

**Test new ideas…**
but <u>never</u> stray too
far away from the
winning formulas
that have been
proven to be the
most successful in
your marketplace.

$ $ $ $ $

# 50 IN 50.

\* \* \* \* \*

**All this talk about
retirement is nonsense!**
Work gives our lives
purpose, meaning, and
structure. Stop telling me
to take it easy... *I'll have
eternity to take it easy!*

\* \* \* \* \*

**50 IN 50.**

The question all marketers
<u>must</u> constantly ask:

# What's next?

# 50 IN 50.

# Jump – and the net will appear!

- √ Make the commitment first.
- √ Set the deadline!
- √ Run the ad – then scramble to put the fulfillment together!
- √ Make <u>BIG</u> <u>PROMISES</u> to groups of customers – and then scramble to make them real!
- √ Do whatever you can to force yourself to do more!

**50 IN 50.**

**Salespeople get paid
to hear the word "no!"**

**A "no" does not
mean "no" to the
aggressive person
who wants the sale!**

**50 IN 50.**

• • • • •

**Take good care of
the people who take
good care of you!**

• • • • •

**50 IN 50.**

```
┌ ─ ─ ─ ─ ─ ─ ─ ─ ─ ─ ─ ─ ─ ─ ─ ─ ┐
│                                  │
│      Your best work              │
│    is still out there!           │
│                                  │
└ ─ ─ ─ ─ ─ ─ ─ ─ ─ ─ ─ ─ ─ ─ ─ ─ ┘
```

# 50 IN 50.

Better to **strengthen your back** than to lighten your load!

**50 IN 50.**

All growth comes from
consciously living outside
of your comfort zone.

If you're not doing things
on a regular basis that scare
you just a little (or a lot!)
– you're not growing.

**50 IN 50.**

# More business problems are created by indecision than bad decision.

*Go ahead and take massive action!* Try many different things and fail and learn from all your mistakes while daring big and failing again and again!

**50 IN 50.**

**Spend <u>more</u> money – to close more sales!**

1. You can't go wrong if you are spending this money on super qualified prospects.
2. You are selling big ticket items with good margins.

In some cases (as long as your percentage of conversion is going up) you can't spend too much money!

# 50 IN 50.

# Most marketers are weak.

* They quit way too soon.
* They are too worried about offending their prospects or customers.
* Or, they simply don't know that there is a great deal more money laying on the table that could and should be theirs – if they simply went after it more aggressively and then stayed after it until they got it!

**50 IN 50.**

Your business is like a
bicycle.  Either you keep it
moving or you fall down!

- Keep searching for your
  next big winner!
- Keep finding better ways
  to give your customers
  and prospects what you
  know they want the most!

**50 IN 50.**

Create as many
"businesses within
your business" as
you possibly can.

50 IN 50.

# Get your *best offer* in front of <u>more people</u> and follow-up like crazy!

# 50 IN 50.

# The best product does not always win, *but the best marketing always does!*

50 IN 50.

\* \* \* \* \* \* \* \* \*

# All business is
# *show business!*

\* \* \* \* \* \* \* \* \*

# 50 IN 50.

# Your best customers are like fires. They go out if unattended.

- The key word is "relationship."

- The better they "feel" about you – the more money they will give you!

- Remember, the fire never dies as long as you keep feeding it!

## 50 IN 50.

Many people think nothing of spending $60,000.00 to put their teenage son or daughter in college for 4 to 6 years so they can become a nameless, faceless middle managers and make enough money to drive a nice car and live in an upper-middle class neighborhood.

**Those same people will totally freak out when asked to cough up $3,000.00 for a marketing seminar that is designed to show them how to make millions of dollars.**

# Why is this?

# 50 IN 50.

# "What are you willing to do?"

The answer to these six words will determine how much money you will ultimately make.

**50 IN 50.**

\* \* \* \* \* \* \* \* \* \*

## Rock star or brain surgeon?

Your time is the most precious
commodity you have. *So why would
you want to sell it for any amount of
money?* <u>Don't</u> <u>do</u> <u>this</u>! Find as many
ways as you can to make money that
have little or even nothing to do with
the amount of time you put into it.

\* \* \* \* \* \* \* \* \* \*

# 50 IN 50.

**What is the best way to deepen your relationship with your customers?**

> The answer: hold seminars, tele-seminars, workshops, and other "training" events that bond with them by showing them that you care and really want to help them.

> You can also do this through the careful creation of all kinds of information products that are sold or sent to them.

**50 IN 50.**

**The only 3 ways to make money:**

1. <u>Sell your time for money</u>.  You charge by the hour and trade your life for a paycheck.

2. <u>Sell a product or service</u>.  Your money comes from the sale of the gizmo – not the time or work it takes to sell it.

3. <u>Passive income</u>.  Your money makes you more money <u>without</u> your direct effort.  All of the world's richest people make their money with the third method.  Their money comes to them automatically from a wide variety of cash-producing investments.  Their money keeps making them more money!  Do everything you can to make as much of your money as possible in the third area!  What would you rather be: A rock star or a brain surgeon?

# 50 IN 50.

# The 9 Major Marketing Mistakes
## *and How to Avoid Them!*

1. **No Focus:** The list of prospects is #1. Hone in on one specific highly qualified prospect. Know them in the most intimate way.

2. **No Compelling Offer:** You must have something hot to get people to take action now!

3. **No Deadline:** The more urgency you can build into your offer – the higher your response rate will be!

4. **No Testimonials:** What other people say about you is much more important than what you say about yourself.

5. **No Measurement of Results:** The only thing that counts is ROI (Return on Investment). Know your numbers! Don't get hung up on response rates.

6. **No Follow-Up:** Most people are giving up on 'em way too soon. Eighty-two percent of sales happen after the first follow-up!

7. **Trying to Be Cute and Funny:** Use direct response (not "Madison Avenue") advertising.

8. **BAD Copy:** The right words rule!

9. **Too Much Reliance on One Media:** Diversify! Multiple legs on table!

**50 IN 50.**

Here is one of my favorite quotes that is right next to my big clock, so I can see it all the time:

"Business is <u>always</u> a struggle. There are always obstacles and competitors. There is never an open road, except the wide road that leads to failure. Every great success has always been achieved by fight. Every winner has scars. Those who succeed are the efficient few. They are the few who have the ambition and willpower to develop themselves."

*Herbert N. Casson*

**50 IN 50.**

# Our greatest rock-n-roll role model is the heavy metal band "AC/DC."

"AC/DC" has recorded nearly 20 albums and sold over 200 million albums worldwide with the same 3 chord songs on each one. The fans don't care! In fact, not giving them the same 3 chords in every song on every album would cause them to stop buying! Their worldwide fan base would dry up immediately!

**Find your formula and, once you do find it, <u>never</u> <u>stray</u> <u>from</u> <u>it</u>!**

**50 IN 50.**

# Hard work is good for your soul.

√ Plus, it may keep you alive longer!

√ And even if it doesn't, it will add more life to your years.

√ "Hard work never killed a man. Men die of boredom, psychological conflict, and disease. Indeed, the harder you work – the happier you will be." *David Oglivy*

√ "Seek above all else a game worth playing and play it as if your entire life and sanity depended on it...for it does!" *Edward DeRopp*

# 50 IN 50.

**More problems = more action!**

## *So bring it on, baby!*

You get rich by consistently doing the things other people cannot or will not do. Taking huge risks, putting your neck on the line, and facing the tremendous struggles (from backing yourself into a corner or tackling more than you can handle) is the secret to creating lots of problems – THAT CAN SPUR YOU ON BIG TIME!

**50 IN 50.**

Delegate your weaknesses.

**Focus on
your strengths.**

# 50 IN 50.

## The 10 main things that made us millions:

1. We knew the market – <u>before</u> we started our business.

2. Previous business experience.

3. Partnership of two very different people.

4. Fell in love with our business.

5. Focused on serving customers.

6. Help from experts.

7. Help from many others!

8. Learned the art and skill of developing products and offers.

9. Learned how to develop front-end and back-end marketing systems.

10. Strived to give our customers <u>MORE</u> than they received from our competitors.

*(From our 10-year anniversary seminar in 1998.)*

# 50 IN 50.

## <u>Never</u> <u>Fear</u> <u>Objections</u>.

Don't hide!  Be upfront
about the skepticism you
know they feel…  Bring up
the biggest objections
yourself.  Then overcome
them one by one.  You'll win
their trust and respect –
and you'll get their money.

*The best prospects have
major objections that
must be faced head-on
and not skated around.*

# 50 IN 50.

> **The pain
> of discipline
> <u>hurts</u> <u>less</u>
> than the pain
> of regret.**

**50 IN 50.**

You have to *roll* with the punches!

Keep getting up – every time you get knocked down.

**50 IN 50.**

# Are all highly-successful entrepreneurs a little crazy?

**Maybe, but one thing is for certain: almost all of them tend to be very creative. The symptoms of creativity are also directly related to insanity! Check it out for yourself:**

| CREATIVITY | MADNESS |
|---|---|
| High energy | Mania, insomnia |
| Heightened senses | Mood disorder |
| Eccentricity | Erratic behavior |
| Emotional expressiveness | Emotional volatility |
| Spontaneity | Impulsiveness |
| Risk taking | Recklessness |
| Single-mindedness | Obsessiveness |
| Unusual perceptions | Distortions of reality |
| Visions | Hallucinations |
| Big ideas | Grandiosity |
| Fluency of ideas | Flight of ideas |
| High standards | Perfectionism |
| Feelings of giftedness | Narcissism |

The more you think about this, you'll realize that all great entrepreneurs definitely have all of the symptoms on the left-hand side of this chart!

# 50 IN 50.

# STOP LOWERING YOUR PRICES!

Low prices are reserved for people who <u>cannot</u> market themselves effectively. If you're competing on price, you haven't established enough value in the minds of your prospective customers. It's up to you to prove – without a doubt – that the best prospective buyers in your market should be giving more of their money to you. Marketing is all about differentiation, but it's up to you to create those perceptions of difference in the minds of the people you most want on your customer list.

# 50 IN 50.

**Strive to be <u>more</u> "human" in all of your communications.**

√ Be real!

√ Be raw!

√ Be imperfect!

*Let them feel what you feel and see the REAL person behind the words they are reading.*

**50 IN 50.**

# Learn by doing.

You can't let a simple thing
like the fact that you've
<u>never</u> done something or
don't know how to do it
stop you from doing it.

The fact that entrepreneurs
are willing to boldly step out
and face the unknown – and
figure it all out as they go – is
the one thing that separates
them from everyone else.

**50 IN 50.**

• • • • •

# The front-end builds your list, but the back-end makes you rich!

• • • • •

**50 IN 50.**

**The #1 reason that the most solid businesses begin to decline is simply because they <u>STOP</u> doing the things that took them to the top.**

- They lose their edge.

- They lose their focus.

- They lose their hunger.

- They lose the boldnees and creativity they had when they were struggling their way to the top. They become conservative and complacent. Now they are easy targets for all of the others who are just like they once were!

# 50 IN 50.

"You <u>can't</u> kill an
elephant with a BB gun!"

*Bill Glazer*

People are trying to get
HUGE results with a small
amount of effort and expense.

**YOU <u>CAN'T</u> DO IT!**

**50 IN 50.**

# SPECIAL
# BONUS
## <u>50</u> SECRETS

# 50 IN 50.

People are looking for and willing to spend a ton of money for:

# <u>The</u> <u>Magic</u> <u>Pill</u>!

This is the product or service that they perceive can instantly and automatically give them something they badly want.

**50 IN 50.**

> Strive to make your offer
> so attractive, compelling,
> and irresistible *that only
> a lunatic would say "No!"*

**50 IN 50.**

# "What people want is a miracle!"

**Gene Swartz**
(One of the World's Greatest
Direct Response Marketing
Copywriters of All-Time)

> People want easy answers and quick solutions.

> People love pat answers – easy solutions – simple ideas – and stuff that sounds good! They want sugar coated bullshit! They like words and ideas that are coated with syrup and sprinkled with sugar!

**50 IN 50.**

# The 4 laws of self teaching:

1. *You are your greatest teacher.*
2. You can learn <u>anything</u> you want to learn.
3. You <u>must</u> take total responsibility for everything that happens to you.
4. Experience + Reflection = Wisdom!

# 50 IN 50.

The great Olympic runner,
Steve Prefontaine said:

"There may be men
who can beat me –
<u>but</u> <u>they'll</u> <u>have</u> <u>to</u>
<u>bleed</u> <u>to</u> <u>do</u> <u>it!</u>"

**50 IN 50.**

• • • • •

# Step out in faith – and figure it out *as you go!*

• • • • •

**50 IN 50.**

**Do everything
possible to shift
the power and get
them to chase you –
*rather than you
chasing them!***

**50 IN 50.**

**P. T. Barnum-ize every offer!**

– Big!
– Blow it up!
– Bold!
– Explosive!
– Wow them!
– History making!
– Whiz-bang!
– Hype it!
– Jazz it up!
– Make it rock!

**50 IN 50.**

# Fight like hell, but choose your battles wisely.

**50 IN 50.**

If the desks are too neat and clean... and the people all look relaxed... the company is in **BIG TROUBLE!!!**

# 50 in 50.

**$ $ $**

# Happiness is...
## a never-ending stream of positive cash-flow!

**$ $ $**

**50 IN 50.**

Retirement = **Death.**

**50 IN 50.**

**Failure** is the best education.

- Test a lot of different things.
- Set out to try bold things (on a small basis).
- And then never repeat what didn't work!
- The more you test – and fail – the better!  Why? Because you will ultimately discover what works best.

**50 IN 50.**

**Stop waiting for inspiration!
Instead, you must get up
every morning with the
determination to press on –
and do creative work – even if
you don't feel like it.  Your
motion will create the emotion.**

"Most of life is routine – dull
and grubby – but routine is
the momentum that keeps a
man going.  If you wait for
inspiration you'll be standing
on the corner after the parade
is a mile down the street."

*Ben Nicholas*

**50 IN 50.**

> You serve yourself
> best – *when you serve
> others the most.*

**50 IN 50.**

## A good swipe file can make you a ton of money!

> Use it to jump-start your thinking.
> Get new creative ideas that you would have never discovered without it.
> It's a brainstorming tool – if you realize that all great selling ideas can be transferred from one product, service, or business to another.
> In other words, the ideas that are or have brought in a ton of money for one person or company can be worth a fortune to you!

# 50 IN 50.

**Sell yourself first. Bond with them. Then sell your stuff!**

√ It's so much easier to sell things to people AFTER you make a strong connection with them.

√ You must break down their sales resistance <u>before</u> you start pitching to them.

√ Honest Abe knew this: "If you would win a man to your cause, first convince him that you are his sincere friend." *Abraham Lincoln*

**50 IN 50.**

# Formal generalized education sucks!

The only thing that's important is specialized knowledge and experience that is directed in a very specific direction.

50 IN 50.

< < < < < <

**Life, love,
and business
favor the bold!**

> > > > > >

**50 IN 50.**

• • • • •

## Love will find a way – indifference will find an excuse.

√ Learn to love the things you do that bring you the largest number of sales and profits!

√ Love makes all burdens light. This is the key to doing your best work!

• • • • •

# 50 IN 50.

71

# "The road to excess leads to enlightenment!"

## *William Blake*
### *(A man who pushed the envelope!)*

√ You <u>never</u> know how far you can go until and unless you push yourself way too far!

√ You push it hard – until it breaks – then fix it – then push it even harder, until it breaks again!

√ Whoever said, "Don't bite off more than you can chew," was wrong! The secret to wealth is to constantly be involved in way more projects than you can possibly handle! You must boldly push beyond your limits in order to expand them. The higher you climb, the more you can see... SO KEEP CLIMBING HIGHER!

**50 IN 50.**

\* \* \* \* \* \* \* \* \* \* \* \* \*

# Whoever owns the BIGGEST and MOST RESPONSIVE mailing list is <u>king</u>!

\* \* \* \* \* \* \* \* \* \* \* \* \*

# 50 IN 50.

The **true art** of selling is to make people feel that they are the ones chasing you!

To be very aggressive with your marketing <u>without</u> appearing like you need or even care whether they do business with you.

**50 in 50.**

# Catch yourself on fire and they will come to watch you burn!

*Winston Churchill said it best:*

"Before you can inspire with emotion, you must be swamped with it yourself."

# 50 IN 50.

• • • • • • • • •

# Wise men have <u>many</u> doubts.

• • • • • • • • •

**50 IN 50.**

Database marketing in 3 words:

1. **Segment**

2. **Concentrate**

3. **Dominate!**

**50 IN 50.**

# Never give up!

*I read somewhere that...*
"Success is the ability to hold on,
long after others have let go."

Like many quotes, it sounded good
so I committed it to memory. But
the longer I am self-employed,
the more I know how true this is!

# 50 IN 50.

# The easy way to dramatically increase your persuasive power: <u>WRITE</u> <u>MORE</u>!

> Consistent writing about your #1 subject helps to crystalize your thinking.

> This, in turn, <u>will</u> make you a much more persuasive thinker. You will speak with greater confidence and power. Your ideas will be sharper and more people will want to buy and re-buy from you.

# 50 IN 50.

# Breakdowns can lead to breakthroughs!

√ Adversity is good for your soul. It builds character. It makes you stronger. It shapes you.

√ Adversity is the great developer of all great entrepreneurs.

**50 IN 50.**

$ $ $

Getting rich <u>and</u> <u>staying</u> <u>rich</u> are two entirely different things.

They require a different set of skills.

$ $ $

# 50 IN 50.

## If you don't know it can't be done, you can do it.

An educated person will stay up all night and worry about things that most of us never even think about. We are too damn busy doing the deal to worry about anything.

**50 IN 50.**

# Your **best** will continue to get better!

√ Stay committed to mastery!
Stay hungry. Continue to learn
all you can. Give each project
everything you've got – and your
best will continue getting better!

√ The real joy of mastery is when
you finally have the ability to do
amazing things...in the most
natural way. To get to the
place where great things seem
to flow out of you in the most
natural way...where all of the
things that were once difficult
are now easy, and even fun!

# 50 IN 50.

&gt; &gt; &gt; &gt; &gt; &lt; &lt; &lt; &lt; &lt;

**The <u>why</u> to do something always
comes before the <u>how</u> to do it!**
*This is the secret behind all great achievers.*

**Great achievers set the goal – and then
figure it out as they go along. You can't
let a little thing like not knowing how
you're going to do something stop you!**

&gt; &gt; &gt; &gt; &gt; &lt; &lt; &lt; &lt; &lt;

**50 IN 50.**

> If you think the way
> you've always thought –
> *you'll get everything
> you've always got!*

# 50 IN 50.

# "Selling is a performance!"

## *Dan Kennedy*

Dan also says that selling <u>is</u> <u>not</u> <u>serving</u>. The root word for serving is "servant." Serving your customer is a vital role in the marketing and customer service area of your business – but not the "selling" side of what you do. Selling is all about control and power over the prospect or customer. You are the one in charge, not them. You are the one who leads them to buy. You must be the one who controls the entire selling process, not them.

# 50 IN 50.

The 10 most powerful
two-letter words in
the English language:

**If it is to be
it is <u>up</u> <u>to</u> <u>me</u>.**

# 50 IN 50.

• • • • •

# Remain
# <u>open</u>,
# <u>flexible</u>,
# and <u>curious</u>.

• • • • •

**50 IN 50.**

Customers go where
they are invited –
and stay where they
are appreciated.

**50 IN 50.**

$ $ $ $ $

The door will
<u>always</u> be open to
the person who can
make money for others.

$ $ $ $ $

**50 IN 50.**

- - - - - - - -

# There's an easy way and a hard way to do something.

Only a fool chooses the hard way just for the sake of doing it hard. The smart person strives to keep it as easy – simple – and manageable as possible.

- - - - - - - -

# 50 IN 50.

— $ $ $ —

## Relationship Marketing:

Win their hearts –
then win their
pocketbooks!

— $ $ $ —

**50 IN 50.**

\* \* \* \* \*

## Always have your <u>next</u> project waiting in the wings!

\* \* \* \* \*

**50 IN 50.**

Problems contain massive
amounts of energy.  The
same problems that kill some
people – cause others to
shoot straight to the top!

The pressure from the
problems should be used to
create the solutions!

**50 in 50.**

Many people are <u>too</u> <u>smart</u> to get rich. Their intelligence is a trap. They use all their mental powers to find and focus on all the obstacles – rather than the outcomes.

**50 IN 50.**

**If you always
think the way you
always thought...
you'll always get what
you've always got!**

**50 IN 50.**

# If your customers want to buy rocks... then start digging!

Most marketers are trying too hard to sell people the things that <u>they</u> want to sell... instead of just selling what their market wants to buy.

Seasoned marketers are the <u>most</u> guilty of this. They believe their marketing skills are powerful enough to sell anything to anyone!

**50 IN 50.**

## Another powerful "secret" from Dan Kennedy.

On Dan's "Renegade Millionaire" program he says:

## "You must work on yourself as hard or even harder than you work on your business."

I instantly pulled my car off the road, wrote this down, and have been thinking about it ever since. You should, too. There is so much truth in this one statement – especially if you have been in business for many years. So many seasoned entrepreneurs tell me in private that they have lost their passion for the business that they once had. I've felt this way, too. When you reach this stage in your entrepreneurial life, working on yourself becomes even more important. *You must keep finding all kinds of ways to fire yourself up and keep the flames burning hot!*

# 50 IN 50.

## $ $ $ $ $

**The more HONEST and OPEN you are with your customers, the more <u>BONDED</u> they will be to you and the more they'll buy!**

People are sick and tired of all the phony-sounding B.S. out there. THEY DON'T TRUST ANYONE ANYMORE. They are looking for something "<u>REAL</u>" and want to have a relationship with you. The more you do to tell them your carefully crafted "personal and private" details, the more money you'll make.

*Try this and prove it to yourself!*

## $ $ $ $ $

**50 IN 50.**

> **When people pay –**
> **they pay attention!**

**50 IN 50.**

# Great Marketers are Hunters.

We are happiest when we're on the hunt.  The bigger the hunt – the happier we are. *We must be reaching all the time.*  All is well as long as our reach exceeds our grasp.

**50 IN 50.**

www.ingramcontent.com/pod-product-compliance
Lightning Source LLC
Chambersburg PA
CBHW022112210326
41521CB00028B/317